The Dreamer and the Dream

by

Rick E. Roberts

Indian Paintbrush Poets

Copyright © 2009 by Rick E. Roberts. All rights reserved.

Published by Indian Paintbrush Poets, an imprint of Pearn and Associates, Inc., Boulder, Colorado. For information about our products and services please contact us at happypoet@hotmail.com,

Cover design by Anne Kilgore.

Acknowledgements

To Jesus for all you have become to me, not just what you do, but who you are. I really am amazed more every day and words seem inferior which, is funny for a writer. I love you more today than yesterday. Thanks for giving me all that you have, and all that you are.

Library of Congress Control Number: 2009933127

Roberts, Rick E. 1965
The Dream and the Dreamer, Rick E. Roberts. First Edition.
ISBN 978-0-9841683-0-9 paper.

This book is dedicated to my wife Melissa, who has been the greatest joy of my life for over thirty years. She is the one who taught me that you could be loved, that you do have value, that there is something more than what the world is offering you. She showed me unconditional love and was the first person I ever trusted. She is gentle and kind, my greatest gift and my best friend. All my days are richer because of her love and her friendship. This is for her and for you. Enjoy!

Contents

If The Ocean *1*
Learning To Obey *2*
Worship Over The Top *3*
I Love To Worship You *4*
After My Son Died *5*
If I Sold My Body *8*
More Peace, More Joy, The More I See *9*
Presumptions of Joy *10*
Be At Last Set Free *11*
Shower Me *12*
Oh Provider *13*
The Hitchhiker *14*
Whispers Of A Hero *16*
Who Will Cry *17*
I Wasn't The Only One *18*
From Fear, So Severe *19*
There Is One *20*
Searching A Long Time *21*
I Am Blessed *24*
He Gave Me Life *25*
Look With Envy *26*
Fresh Paper *27*
Be Still My Restless Heart *28*
I'm Just A Number *29*
The Mind Of A Madman *30*
The Temple *32*
For Your Love *33*
All Over Me *34*
Promises *35*
Fill Me Up *36*
Hold Out Your Hand *37*
My Pain *38*
Hungarian Women *39*
That Book of Matthew *40*
Beauty Is In Everything *42*

Complexities of Genius *43*
Tender Heart Strings *46*
This Black Man *47*
Save Me Jesus *49*
Genuine Tears *51*
New Clothes *52*
Looking Back *53*
Here For You *54*
We Are All To Blame (Columbine) *55*
Paul's Story *57*
I'll Be There When Disaster Comes *59*
To Do Something Remarkable *60*
When I'm Dead *62*
Ask My Savior *63*
No Father, No Son *64*
The Things I Say *65*
Bride Of Haarlem *66*
Testimony *67*
Don't Kill Me Daddy *69*
Donna's Story *70*
Dreams Pass Away *71*
Kitty's Song *72*
Own Feelings *73*
Light In My World *74*
Peace *75*
Never Entered The Truth *76*
Gathers His Own *77*
Cloudy Skies *78*
For The Love Of God Won't Wait *79*
Joseph's Song *80*
Catfish Are Great Listeners *81*
Revelation 'Round The Mountain *82*
Dangers Come To Stay *83*
Say A Prayer To The Lord *84*
Soldiers Unknown *85*
So We Could Learn Of Love *86*
My Mother's Other Son *87*
Each Alone Must Choose *88*

The Thread *89*
From My Window *90*
The Battle *91*
Jappy And Me *93*
Two Way Street *94*
As Midnight Strikes *95*
Does She Get *97*
Don's Legacy And Story *99*
Sun Lee's Story *100*
Spongy Lungs *101*
Stars That Shine *102*
Voices On The River *103*
Just A Dream *104*
Seed Of Knowledge *104*
The Roadhouse Grill *106*
My Heart Is Open *107*
The Benediction *108*

The Dreamer and the Dream

If The Ocean

If the ocean were a well of ink deep within the earth
And everyone alive a writer by trade, by choice or birth.
And all the land and sky above
Were as paper for us to write
Then how could we begin to tell of God's love and light?
We'd drain the ocean dry, as we wrote across the sky
Of the love that God is, until we went to be with Him.
And we'd fall far short, as we wrote our report
Writing all about God and His love,
All He is and all He's done.

Learning To Obey

Learning to obey, to accept the joy that comes
The joy He wants to give when we visit Him as sons.
Learning to believe that everyone has merit
And love never runs cold, if you take it out and share it.
Learning to remember the part I left behind
And knowing someone else
Needs to seek the Lord and find.
Learning to be patient when I feel the urgency
Trusting God's timing always,
He waited 23 years for me!
Learning to make time to be with God alone
To pray and fast for Him and make His power known.
Learning to trust Him for my place in His plan
Whether I do the one thing or be like Billy Graham.
Learning to change my ways in the little tiny things
With motives pure and a heart clean,
A process never ending.

Worship Over The Top

Praise the Lord of heaven, let's worship Him tonight
He'll make this night sanctified,
Bathed in His holy light.
Put His Spirit deep inside me, give Him all my praise
Lift up His name on high He's worthy to be raised.
His word is like a river, I'm gonna get my fill
He'll take me to His throne tonight, in humility I will.
Love and serve, all His children, obey His holy call
I want to change my heart tonight, give the Lord my all.
Set this place on fire, yes the Holy Spirit will
Praise you Father, Precious Son, come Holy Spirit fill.
Thank you Lord and Savior, forgiving us our sins
Praise you Lord to greet us when we come to you again.
Thank you for this moment to worship you O Lord
Teach us to pray and serve,
Apply your word, our sword.
Put our boasting in you only, throw away our pride
It only happens when you Lord come live in us inside.
Thank you for discernment, you've given to each child
A chance to choose the way
We should instead of going wild.
Let our hearts beat for you Father, you alone are true
Lead us to a holy place, full of grace from you.

I Love To Worship You

I could never sing for fortune and fame
I couldn't sing at all, but you called and I came.
I don't care if anyone watches, it's only me and you
I stand for you, I pray to you, I love to worship you.
Oh Lord, you are my peace and joy always
If it is your will, let me sing to you in this way.
With no fear, no notes, no sound, all I feel is you
As my heart pours out,
I cry to you, I'm bound forever true.
I could never carry a tune in a bucket or a box
That's before you came
And showed me how, Jesus rocks!
Jesus Rocks! The world! Everyone's invited to see
His love is real and it's alive, coming to life in me.
I have no song to sing, no precious gift to bring
Only to the cross, I cling,
Give my all, my everything, to sing.
With no fear, no notes, no sound, all I feel is you
As my heart pours out,
I cry to you, I'm bound forever true.

After My Son Died

I did drugs everyday,
Tried everything to take the pain away
After my son died,
I found a bottle and crawled inside.
I tried topless dancers and cocaine whores
Marijuana, LSD and waking up on the floor.
But after my son died,
The one I prayed would come
I looked at my life and said, "What have I done?"
I turned and yelled at God,
I knew He was still there
And I poured out my angry, bitter heart,
After years of despair.
And He listened, oh my God, He Listened.
I told Him about my dad and my mom and alcohol
And the years I spent alone and He had tried to call.
I couldn't hear him or I just, didn't want to
I knew He was there,
But not enough to let Him through.
And I told Him all I did as the tears flowed out
How some days I wanted to die
And everyday I had doubts.
I was supposed to be a king, hey!
What was happening?
Was it only a dream I had,
I screamed at my real dad.
I didn't know Him then, but He was listenin'
The more I cried, the more I asked why,
The more He says I love you child.
He quieted my heart and told me an old story
About another son that died,
Being killed after beaten gory.
But I have a plan He said to let the world return
To the beauty I have always meant,

But will they ever learn?
I've heard your cries,
And I looked down on your sleeping
And every time you ran away,
You wound up sad and weeping.
I waited for you for 22 years to take one step my way
And always watched you very close,
Until that moment came.
You cried to me the one who made you,
Perfect as you are
And you're more precious than anything,
This old world or any star.
After my Son died,
The Lord Jesus Christ is His name
He paid the price for sin's demise
And for three days He remained.
Separated from me so that all
The world was redeemed
If only they would trust my word
And let Him reign supreme.
Yes I called you to be a king to wear
A golden crown
To live a life fighting for truth
And never backing down.
To be hated, scorned and mocked,
Like the prophets who were before you
To die for me, a martyr, a son,
Here's what I will do.
I will never leave, forget you or forsake you,
Always love and care for you
Fill you with my Holy Spirit
And pour out your blood if I need to.
I stopped to think
And softly I said thank you
There's nothing else I'd rather do
Than bleed and die for you.
So use me as you will,

I am bought, sold and paid for
And show me all that I must suffer,
All that I was made for.
Like Paul, Peter, Joshua, Moses, Elijah, Stephen,
Sampson, Ruth, Boaz, David and Messiah!
Born to die so they might live,
The ones who hate His hope
Kill me if I can keep someone
Else's neck from the rope.
The same one I had my neck in,
All those years ago
Thanks for cutting me free,
Good Savior, sin wouldn't let me go.
Until we let God do it all, we'll never live truly
If you let Him, He will help you,
Set you free to see.
Take one step His way,
Fifteen years ago I did it
He will meet you where you are,
He will help you quit it.
All the wrong things,
All the wrong thoughts
All the wrong motives
And running from the cops.
I did it all wrong, my whole life, so long
I hope you can see, what He's done for me,
Teaching me this song.
To trust Him all the day long,
Go to Him to be strong
Be free from sin, His power within,
His Holy Spirit belongs, in you.

If I Sold My Body

If I sold my body for sexual sin,
Uncovering my shame over and over again
And after, I felt I had died within,
Jesus came to wash me, now I win!
If I gave myself to be all used up,
For someone's lust, not someone's love
When I hated the harlot I had become,
Jesus came to marry me, now we are one.
Don't say that I'm a prostitute, I did what I did,
But here's the new truth
When I hated that feeling, I'm a piece of meat,
Jesus came to save me, now I'm complete.
Go to Jesus, run to Jesus, pray to Jesus and live!
Let's go to Jesus, cry to Jesus, run to Jesus, He lives!
We all want the redemption, only Jesus can give!
To live for real, not the way that I've lived!

More Peace, More Joy, The More I See

I can see Elijah waving goodbye,
Chariot of fire, he goes into the sky
I can see Daniel running free,
A furnace fiery, with his integrity
I can see Moses on his face,
Seeking grace, in God's holy place
I see Abraham, knife in hand to
Slay his son, but then, God rescued him
I see David dancing like a quark,
Before the Ark, before the Lord
I can see myself in Psalm 51,
O what have I done, crucified God's Son.
So the more I see, the more I want to be like Jesus
The more I do, the more I run to you my Jesus
You are no sinking sand, take me by the hand,
Before I go and blaspheme you again.
I see Paul on the Damascus road,
Anger explodes, then God comes close
Shows him all he must suffer
To make him tougher, to endure the load.
I see Peter walking on the waves,
Defies the grave, but then Jesus saves
I see myself growing day by day,
Learning to pray, learning to gray.
I can see Jesus on the throne,
His love is shown, for His own
I can see Jesus a tear in His eye,
The cost is high, He will pay the price
I see John the Baptist by the river,
Baptizing believers, that God will deliver
I can John his head on a platter,
His blood splattered, a martyr forever.
More peace, more joy, the more I see.

Presumptions Of Glory

Presumptions of glory, excesses of pride
Pour out from me when I'm wounded inside.
I know nothing further and lately I know less
When I think I understand it, I make a bigger mess.
So I fight and I wrestle with the God who makes me real
Instead of peace where I nestle
And His goodness I can feel.
I find myself in conflict, but God can make it new
It's about waiting on Him, not anything I can do.

Be At Last Set Free

Please remember what is,
All that can be and what's gone
Be at last set free to run and to walk along.
Nowhere near over is the life of pain and tears
But mercy reigns, and plans
Reveal to overcome our fears.
Please remember what is and be grateful for all of it
Use no cross words or desperate pleas,
Never give up or quit
Nowhere near over is the life of pain and tears
But mercy reigns, and plans
Reveal, to overcome our fears.
Sometimes it takes years.

Shower Me

Shower me in your cleansing love,
Wash me in your mercy flood
Until my eyes can see for real,
Until my hands can touch and feel
Until my peace is beyond all,
Until my ears can hear your call.
I'm dirty, prone to sin, I'm filthy,
Wandering off again
To find where demons dwell to
Live my life like hell, but I yell
God I love you, please deliver me from death,
In a whisper I feel your breath
In a vapor, your presence blessed,
In a moment, your care and tenderness
Save me, seek me from the road I'm on,
Shake me make me come back, when I've gone.
I'm foolish in making choices,
I'm tarnished, I could be rejoicing
Nothing is more than you,
No one more true than you
Leading me through, helping me do,
All you want me to do!
Shower me in your cleansing love,
Wash me in your mercy flood
Until my eyes can see for real,
Until my hands can touch and feel
Until my peace is beyond all,
Until my ears can hear your call.
Because you're here and
In a whisper I feel your breath
In a vapor, your presence blessed,
In a moment, your care and tenderness
Save me, seek me from the road I'm on,
Shake me make me come back, when I've gone.
I don't want to be gone anymore.

Oh Provider

Oh provider, provide life for me,
Great provision, your love sets me free
All my urgency, is a gift, from you,
I want to, go as far, as you need me to.
In love and a purity of heart,
In peace with truth like a dart
The whole, menu of God, not religion ala carte,
I want to go and break their chains apart!
I hope it's acceptable, to the one who made me
To the Son who saves me, I hope it's respectable.
In joy and your perfect will,
In strength and meekness to be still
The whole armor of God, to defend and not to kill,
I want to stand, all His glory to fulfill.
Hallelujah, He reigns, when it pours He reigns
When it's dry He reigns, Hallelujah, He reigns

The Hitchhiker

He said, "Can I get a lift?" and I said,
"Sure, why not man"
Maybe he'll take the gift to
Go where only Jesus can.
"Hope the weather holds, it's a long hard road."
No detours and no delays, Jesus has His own ways.
To draw us in and to draw us out,
Show us what life is about
Pull us near and hold us dear,
Take away our doubt and fear.
"Where are you heading to?" I said.
"To find a meal and a warm bed"
God gives me an opportunity,
To bless this man like he did for me.
I said, "You can come and live with us,
On a ranch we bought for Jesus!
Its work but it is fun, you can be like my son."
The guy just rode in silence,
Remembering his father's violence
The scars and the pain he couldn't go through again.
I saw his lip quiver as he spoke,
"But, I've got no money, I'm broke."
He closed his eyes and sighed.
It was too soon to decide.
So I told him a father's story,
Maybe he thought it was me
God took my words and the traveler heard,
"I love every lost and lonely bird.
There is nothing you can do, to make me not love you
No where you can run, I'll be there for you son.
I'll help you work through it all,
Whatever it takes, we all must fall
To our face and to our knees
To beg God please, take the keys."
He dropped his head a little more,

Laid his hand on the pick-up door
He finally turned to look and speak,
As tears rolled down his cheek.
"I'm afraid. I know I'm not right or true.
All these things you told me to do
How can I trust someone I can't see?
It sounds good, but it's beyond me.
So I told him about my life now,
How He restored my purpose and how
He brought it out and made it new.
A long hard road for a chosen few.
Will you accept God's opinion
That you need forgiveness for sin?
I need it too, we all do.
Try it His way, let's pray it through.
So we bowed and confessed sin together and
Asked God to heal us forever
To give us a lift, it's His perfect gift.
A father and a son set, and God's not done yet.

Whispers Of A Hero

Whispers of a hero, coming up and out to hear
Endless call for a time's birth coming into place is near.
Echoes of a glory, long ago jaded and now faded
Marching ever closer to the now,
When your glory is restored.
When courage is required for sacrifice and more
When good men are inspired,
Seeking, crying on the floor.
When daily hearts are opened,
To learn and turn to truth
When corpses stacked for slaughter,
Come to life and filled with hope then,
All the earth will turn to see, His glory on the clouds
And every sword laid down,
Like humbled hearts once proud.
Then He will remember, the ones who loved and prayed
Who took the time to know him,
whether emperor or slave.

Who Will Cry

O Lord, you are our Father,
We the clay and you the potter
We are the work of your hand,
Help us to understand.
Please don't be angry anymore
Or remember our sin forever
We are your people forgive us,
So we can be together.
Who will cry for the little boy,
Lost, alone and afraid?
Who will cry for the old man
And the decisions that he made?
Who will cry for the young man,
His whole life there before him?
Who will cry for the old man as
His eyes are growing dim?
Who will cry for the little boy
With no daddy of his own?
Will he be a daddy too in the years
When he has grown?
Who will cry with that man,
When he longs to talk to his dad?
Who will cry with that man
When his memories make him sad?
Who will cry for the little boy
Looking up into daddy's face?
The only dad he will ever need
Is with him, full of grace.

I Wasn't The Only One

I wasn't the only one crying, you were there too
Sobbing and sighing with me that's
What I love about you.
When I was lost and lonely, you got me through
I didn't know you then that's
What I love about you.
Real love it's hard to explain,
Real love is coming again
Real hope, real life for free,
How it's meant to be.
I wasn't finding my purpose,
The thing I just had to do
You were there to listen that's
What I love about you.
I wasn't ready to die,
You show me that I have to
If I want to see real life that's
What I love about you.
Real love it's hard to explain,
Real love is coming again
Real hope, real life for free,
How it's meant to be.

From Fear, So Severe

Free me from myself
Alive from thoughts and doubts
From fear so severe,
It prevents motion, paralyzed.
Free me from the past,
From pain and lonely nights
From self-medicating bites
That never really last.
Free me from this world,
With all its selfish hate
And its lustful after taste,
My stomach curdles and curls.
Free me from the lies,
The enemy has laid out
So everyone fades and doubts,
The glory of the Most High.
Free me from the sorrow,
That I bear with everyone
I turn them to the Son,
For a brighter hope tomorrow.
Free me from earthly ties,
I love my freedom in Christ
Keep me humble and wise,
Until I meet you in the sky.

There Is One

Now I am His, yes He is mine,
Oh what love, glory divine
Once full of sin and constant doubt,
A prison strong, with no way out.
But there is one, who holds the keys,
He hears my cries and deepest pleas
Him I will trust, in Him alone,
King of all Kings, upon His throne.
There's broken hearts, in every place,
Waiting for courage and for grace
To come and see, and show us strong,
A life with God where we belong.
In all His love, He draws me near,
Cleans my heart, and quells my fears
Yes there is one, who holds the keys,
He hears my cries and deepest pleas
Him I will trust, in Him alone,
King of all Kings, and Lord of Lords.
So come to him, call on his name,
Let Him in to your life today
Take His hand and walk with Him,
All the way home to heaven.

Searching A Long Time

You've been searching a long time,
But now I've got your attention
So come and sit down a while,
I've been waiting for you and your smile.
You see I was there when you came into life,
I watched you grow through every stage
And when your birth day came,
I was there to cheer you on,
Welcome you into this new world.
Though you had to cry to take that first breath,
I was there to wipe away your tears
I whispered in your ear, so only you could hear,
I love you and I always will.
Yes your parents would fight, sometimes late at night,
You were scared but not alone
My peace around you shone,
A light of hope and not a darkening fright.
Father your love was always there,
Why did I think you didn't care
My heart was hard too young,
I have just begun to
Break the chains and finally be free.
When they got divorced,
And shook you off your course,
I was there in force, to protect you
From guns and step dads too,
From men you never knew
I was and am the only dad that's true,
The only one to be there for you.
Then you moved where mountains dwell
And from those heights you fell
Into drugs and sex and sin,
I was still there too, watching over you
To keep you safe, but I let you see, that life,

if not from me, it won't, it never sets you free.
My son I've been here all along,
when you are weak and strong,
doing good or barely alive
No one else can save you,
I'm the one who made you,
I can restore it too and give you real life.
So you moved in with a girl,
Then moved around the world,
Looking for peace you never found
I prayed to you a prayer that
She could have my child
You heard and she conceived,
She aborted and I grieved,
Determined now to just go wild.
So much deep sorrow in my heart,
Everything gone and torn apart,
I cried until there was nothing left
You gave me life and breath and somehow
Helped me through David's death.
Later on I wrecked another car
And a walk to work was far,
But it's just what you had in mind
To show me who you are,
You listen and wait, never mock or hate,
Patiently you drew me in
Pulled me out and forgave my sin,
Ran the race so I could win.
Like a brand new baby boy,
Freshly washed and full of joy,
Free from things that sin controls,
your love made me whole again.
So salvation comes and it's great,
I grow and celebrate,
But then comes the need to sanctify
Taking out all of that trash,

My life and deeds of the past,
To make room for Jesus
But I must be pure, sanctify me so
My diseases are cured, at your word.
So years roll by and I see
The changes God makes in me,
He gave me a wife, a home and more
He makes all things new, fully restored,
I've learned to reach out to others,
Sharing Christ with sisters and brothers,
Gives them hope like He gives me,
To cut their ropes and set them free.
So each big issue is raised,
It's exhausting but God be praised,
I'm becoming real, feel what I feel,
Not someone else's baggage or terror
Or doubts, it's hard but God works it all out.
Then come the big ones, the place I am still
With no earthly dad
And my children were killed
I've buried four and a part of myself,
Our marriage is tough,
So is our health, but we stay together,
Many storms we weather,
Knowing God can and He will.
I saw you jumping through hoops to get a son,
I used you to get the right parents for a little girl
She was never meant for you,
She will bless everyone with her smile
And curls, all she will do,
She's a blessing counted to you,
Because you went through,
And stayed true and took the pain
She could have endured, when you
Didn't want to and I'm so proud of you.
Here's a son, yes, one for you!

I'm Blessed

My life was going too far in reverse,
Disappointment and scars, what a mess
Then I met Him, He took me in,
Now all I know is I'm blessed.
He took me out of many bad habits,
All too numerous to list
Things in my past, the wisdom that I lacked,
He washed it all away and I'm blessed.
He works in my heart and works in my mind,
To change all my ways into His
Takes me for a ride as He changes me inside,
It's always an adventure, I'm blessed.
The more we go deeper and He shows me myself,
The more I regret what I missed
To live life better, free from every fetter,
Only by His will, truly blessed.

He Gave Me Life

This is a song for my Lord and Savior
He changed my heart and my mind's behavior.
He'll do the same if you love Him truly
Ask for His help and fulfill your duty.
He gave me life, for His praise and pleasure
Now I live with Him forever
Once He was dead, but He's alive, Jesus Christ.
Paid the price, so do what He say
Jesus is the truth and the way
Now I can live since He's alive, Jesus Christ.
This is the truth that the Lord has shown me
I gave Him my life, He bought and owns me.
I was a slave, He's given me real freedom
So I could serve more and bless and love Him.
He gave me life, for His praise and pleasure
Now I live with Him forever
Once He was dead, but He's alive, Jesus Christ.

Look With Envy

Why do I see with anger, when I should be full of joy?
Why do I look with envy at parents with a little girl or boy?
Why do I shake my head as every car goes by?
Why do I open my wallet, close it, then deeply sigh?
Why do I pour out pride instead of a little love?
Why do I carry a weight that crushes me from above?
Why do I lust after power, when I could be content?
Why do I watch television, to see beauty and lament?
Why do I hate teenagers, those who are young and free?
Why do I listen to music and wonder what could be?
Why do I even make friends in a world so cold and gray?
Why do I try to help them, they never hear a word I say?
Why do I dream of a mansion, near a mountain or a beach?
When a mansion with God forever, is easily within my reach.

Fresh Paper

There's a fresh pad of paper at the table where I sit
Waiting with a pen and ink
For someone's words to fall on it.
It's white and clean and recycled with horizontal lines
And every empty piece a poem or symphony in time.
No one knows the future, what will happen next
The paper's ready and waiting,
Do great things no one expects.

Be Still My Restless Heart

Your love is a promise given, your grace is a song
Your peace is a river that carries me along.
My eyes are open, but I can't see you
I'm content and coping until the day I do.
Be still my restless heart, to hear God's holy voice
Keep me close and draw me apart
To pray more and rejoice.
Your love is a promise given, your grace is a song
Your peace is a river, that carries me along.
To a place I've never been, I need to be in touch
I hear you at the ocean, I love you Lord so much.
So meet me in the water, even meet me in the air
The center of earth is hotter, I know you're even there.
My eyes are open, but I can't see you
I'm content and coping until the day I do.
What a day that will be when I see you face to face
And all I say is "Holy" as I marvel at your grace.

I'm Just a Number

My name doesn't matter anymore,
I'm just a number, 60197
I guess I'll never go restored, to be with God in heaven.
Here I am a nobody, I have to do what I'm told
If I do it poorly, I could end up in the hole.
Where the time passes slow
And there's no reason to smile
There's a dimly lit glow, I see two ants on a tile.
I wonder which one could win a sprint race?
When they are all done, I'm alone in this place.
Other inmates would bet to see which ant would win
I guess I'd rather forget, my life, my shame, my sin.
All the things I hate, the death, the worthless scum
I never thought, now contemplate,
What I hated most I have become.
Oh the agony of life now, gray walls are closing in
There is no way or no how I'm ever getting out again.
I've made a giant mess, the over-used bad bus
Someone said I would be blessed
If I just accepted Jesus.
So who is this man? This Son that God loved and gave
What a strange plan, God, to raise him from the grave.
To beat Satan and death and this battle is won
There is one thing left behind, God's offer to everyone.
To live, holy, forever, redeemed, fully and clean
God shows His treasure, our sins soon unseen.
But I've done too much, how could He forgive me?
I'm a dirty such and such,
But His blood can set me free?
The gift of God is simply so, for anyone to receive
It sounds too easy I know, all we do is believe.
The difference comes right then,
The Holy Spirit comes in
He changes what you have been,
And then the adventure begins.

The Mind Of A Madman

See the world through new eyes,
Ask the questions you're seeking
Keep the answers close when the questions change
You can ask them all again.
And see the truth in play, even if they twist it twice
You will understand when you see with new eyes.
Spouting off about things you know,
No one seems to care or know
Enough to make you show an interest,
Share what you have learned bestowed.
They act so sly and sure, but deep things are a blur
Because they never dig to dig,
To become stronger and big.
They themselves know or think they do,
Dismissing your insanity to push you down
They can go up, but only get around on broken legs
Of sadness, lost, fallen, broken crowns
Only you can fit this calling to journey deeper still
Seeking all the finer things even knowing time will kill.
All the doubts so unrelenting,
All the truth so hard to see
All the aching, wandering, hardened lives,
Lived right out before me.
Even things that used to matter are
Changed and still will be untrue
And every turn will be a road of things I just have to do.
But you can't put the must on me as though you
Alone were right for this
All the doing I must do is given
Freely without the consequences.
Things of life will come and go,
Never owning up to be real
I can love when I want to, it's enough to speak
To breathe to think to feel.
I set aside my mind today, it's busy,

Oh it's painful and yet
The more I think, the deeper I go,
The harder then to forget.
The dreams and passions, all the rest,
The oozing wounds of life
The fibers of each one I met,
Leave a spot on my soul, at best
At worst, a darker harder place, full of grief and strife.
I alone am left undaunted, to sort out what it all means
The thoughts that taunt me as I sleep
And fill my haunted dreams.
See my eyes once new again,
Crosshairs for the truth
Watch the bottles flying by to
Break on my face and my tooth.
Another poem sent to say what only words can
But digging deep is never easy,
It takes a special man.
No drugs or pills can take me there,
No substance of this earth
No Einstein bait,
No love or hate,
Not even virgin birth.

The Temple

Walk into the temple in my guilt and shame
Falling on your mercy Lord
To make me whole again.
I'm a sinner sanctified, when you live in me
Wholly justified because your
Blood has set me free.
In the temple, my body is your temple
And I'm falling on my knees, please.
Just to praise you, any way to thank you
The Spirit's alive, He lives inside.
This time at the temple, your Spirit is on fire
Preaching, teaching all your
Truth with passion and desire.
Oh, to know you more, a deeper walk of faith
Obedient in every way, in every time and place
In the temple, my body is your temple
And I'm falling on my knees, please.
Where shall we go, where should we go Lord?
You already have the words of life.
Where shall we go, where should we go Lord?
Let your Spirit flow, overflow.

For Your Love

My Jesus He died on an old wooden cross,
Poured out His blood for our sin
He made the way, we come back to God,
Make us new again, O Lord, make us new again.
He came to bring mercy and re-unite
Lost sinners with peace and grace,
He is humble and loving, He even raised the dead,
So much glory that I have to hide and
Worship Him on my face.
I met Him one day on an old Missouri road,
When I was dead inside, I told Him my story,
He took the load, He changed my heart
And my mind that day,
Held His arms open wide.
His victory is won! So praise His name!
Let all the earth rejoice!
Let us sing, praises to our king,
Thank you Jesus for your love,
Your love, thank you Lord for your love.

All Over Me

All over me, all over me
I've got the blood of an innocent
Man all over me.
He came to earth before He
Appeared in flesh
He was there with three Hebrew
Boys in a fiery furnace
You can choose to obey Him and
you can choose to betray Him
You can rejoice that He bled, and died over you.
Jesus He taught the truth
That had never been heard
He's the way, the truth, the life;
The lamb and the Word.
You can choose to believe Him
And you can choose to receive Him
You can rejoice that He bled,
And died over you.
When He died He was laid in a
Rich man's tomb, rich man's tomb
He was raised from death to life
And He's coming back soon.
You can choose to love Him
Or you can try to rise above Him
You can rejoice that He bled, and died over you.
Jesus, He is all that I ever need,
He paid the price for my
Sin, my lust and greed.
You can choose to accept Him
Or you can choose to reject Him
You can rejoice that He
Respects you enough to decide
You can rejoice that He bled, and died over you.
All over me, all over me
I've got the blood of an innocent man all over me.

Promises

He will cover you, with His presence
And all of His praise
He will lift you up and fill you up
So your heart and soul will sing.
He gave you Jesus, Savior and king
To save you, to change you
To bless you all of your days.
His justice comes, with His mercy,
the gift of life, given freely
Our hope and light, and our safety,
His righteousness, makes me holy.
He will offer you, His splendor,
And all of His peace
Slow down and quiet you, restore your life,
And allow the Spirit's release.
Come Holy Spirit, our counselor
And Lord, He lives in you now
Reveals life! His word is your sword!
His justice comes, with His mercy,
the gift of life, given freely
Our hope and light, and our safety,
His righteousness makes me holy.
He will cover you, with His presence
And all of His praise
He will lift you up and fill you up so
Your heart and soul will sing.

Fill Me Up

Fill me up, to help me stand,
Keep me pure, by your command
A holy race, that I can win,
I seek your face, let me begin.
To love you God, with no fear,
No doubts inside, no alibis just
A pure heart, to know you more,
Help me serve you, until I'm used up.
In the glory of your presence,
I find joy alone
In the peace, of your beauty,
I find rest, bring me home.
Let my love, be real for you,
Let my motives, all be true
Keep me full as you fill me up to
Spill your love into others cups.

Hold Out Your Hand

Hold out your hand, someone needs it
To get them up to walk right through it.
Hold out your heart, it's big enough for two
Someone needs to see that you love them too.
Don't be afraid to try, let the compassion flow
To the one who's lonely or just feeling low.
Just show them by your every action
They are not forgotten and, what satisfaction.
So open, up the doors, show them a better course
Let their hearts be changed by love, not by force.
Hold out today, the hope for that one
Who is afraid of the future that's only just begun.

My Pain

He uses my pain for someone else's gain
He will let me bleed to help saints in need.
He lets me suffer so I can be tougher
He breaks me down and then spreads me around.
I'm just like dust; I have to earn His trust
Even if I have to die, He will be glorified.
He takes my hurt and keeps me alert
So I can be His son, to get His work done.
If I get bruised, I won't be confused
When I am beaten, I know I'm not forgotten.
When I get stoned and they break my bones
I will pour out my soul as the world takes its toll.
God is on His throne, He will call me home
But until it's time to go, I must endure and grow.
To bleed, to bruise and cry, only never asking why
Jesus Christ suffered deeply; it's no different for me.

Hungarian Women

Hungarian women are so beautiful
That everyone should see
The smiling eyes and shier smiles looking back at me.
They have so many races drawn in their bloodlines
All the good genes mixing, that's why they look so fine.
They're interesting to talk to,
About health or wealth or food
Seeing them in person can do any young man good.
But see beyond the beauty, it's more than looks alone
Making Hungarian women desirable
In a way all their own.
Beauty, talent, brains and love,
But she needs a man who cares
Who will court her everyday,
Take her heart and hold her chairs.
Taking her for dinners out,
Bringing her roses just because
Hold her tight and kiss her right,
The romance she is worthy of.
Forever she will love you,
Give you children, make a home
And love you pure with passion,
So your heart will never roam.
Keep the fires burning in her heart
And in your mind
Be thankful for the gift you have,
The best you'll ever find!

That Book Of Matthew

I don't know anything, but Jesus made me different
It was no earthquake or angel choirs,
Here's my testament.
I read the book of Matthew after my son David died
Then my life was over, I wanted to stop the pain inside.
In the book of Matthew, I read about Jesus,
A name I had heard somewhere
He was kind and healed the blind,
I was in despair and He met me there.
I asked a lot of questions, but I didn't call Him Lord
I got madder and sadder, but Jesus held the cord.
Tied around my neck,
I put there myself through sinfulness
And fears and doubt,
I knew nothing of the Lord's holiness.
I talked to Him some more as
I read another chapter
God started to heal me more,
Than any drug or laughter!
And in His book I saw something,
Like a plan made out for us
Made free, to help anybody,
Anyone born again through Jesus.
Made brand new, brought from the darkness,
Bought out of death and hell
And the price has already been paid,
Jesus saved this world that fell.
Jesus made, a way for me,
If I accept Him and His death on Calvary
A free choice where to spend eternity,
but He leaves that up to me.
I keep that book close and every time
I read, I remember a broken Savior
Oh His blood He had to bleed to pay

For my wild, erratic behavior.
It's not just a book or a story;
It's a powerful living thing
Set by God, on earth to teach us
All about abundant living.
Jesus is the way to the Father's blessings
Prayer is the key so there is no guessing.
And works don't mean a thing,
Apart from knowing God himself
Just let me know you God,
I want to learn to be like you myself.

Beauty Is In Everything

Waterfalls and rainbows shine,
Like crystals in this heart of mine
Beauty is in everything, imagine
Seeing it all from the beginning.
Shadow boxes, grains of sand,
holding this world inside your hand
Seashells with a story to tell,
Like every coin in the wishing well.

Complexities Of Genius

Jesus came over for a cup of tea,
He said some interesting things to me
He told me my problem, he could cure
To change my heart to be pure.
So I took in all He said in and went
Off to go sledding again
He was there at once,
close to me after I almost slammed into a tree.
So I had Him over for dinner
And He told me I was a sinner
I knew He was right
In all He said that stormy night.
But I took off to Hollywood to
go revel in my folly real good
When I looked I saw Him again, in Vegas?
Among all this sin?
I said, "You are persistent, but why?"
He said, "You're needed or millions will die!"
I said, "I'm not responsible, just an ordinary guy
and hardly noticeable, so why?"
He said, "I will help you to make this all come true.
You are the one required,
But you must quit the choir."
"Hey wait I love to sing,
Why should I give up everything?
I'm supposed to solo on Sunday,
How about some other day?"
The time was chosen, it was meant,
Giving me a divine appointment
But I ran the other way too fast
And began thinking on my past.
I thought I'm no good and I waited,
Much too long, so I was fated
To fail when God called as I sat all around and stalled.
What did you want me to do then,

I didn't condemn those men!
The truth came and it scared me,
But God didn't spare me.
He made it so plain I'd get it,
I needed to pray in the closet
"But that's too easy," I said,
"Where's the terror and the dread?"
Funny, God doesn't always say Africa
Or raise the dead like Tabitha
I wasted a huge chance
Chose myself within a selfish glance.
I remembered His call for awhile,
And then I hoped with a smile
Nothing bad would happen soon,
But I found out that afternoon.
An earthquake killed my friend
Tommy and created a giant tsunami
So I cried and I wailed, I chose to hide,
I have failed!
So little was asked of me to help
Prevent the tragedy
In the closet I would pray,
Listening to God only now to obey.
How easy for God to take away,
The suffering of that day
But I was too old, too busy, too sick,
Too slow, worried, just too thick!
To let anything change my mind
And 100,000 orphans were left behind
Now I sit and I beg aloud
For God to turn this thing around.
A long time has passed since,
The Lord was able to convince
Me of His powers all purposeful,
His bond of love unbreakable.
He never forces His way in,
We have to freely choose Him!
Sometimes I still want to run,

but I remember what's been done.
How powerful a prayer can be
And it's hard to run from a tsunami
It's important to serve God's will
To serve Him well and still.
What would have been,
If I had done it back then?
Ask yourself this minute,
There's the closet, are you in it?

Tender Heart Strings

Your forehead is cold while
Your hands are crossed
The same look I saw
On your face is not lost.
I fall when I start to
Remember your smile
I recall in my heart,
You made it all worthwhile.
We admire the way you said
What you meant
Always cherish the time
And the joy that we spent.
With you and your husband,
All the good you have born
And our tender heart strings,
Once tied are now torn.
But we're hopeful to see you,
We will soon again
You're there and we will
Be with God in heaven.

This Black Man

You've hated me my whole life,
But we've never met
You find me repulsive,
Like a criminal and yet . . .
I feel like showing you,
I'm not like what you see
Blame my fathers for the hate
They tried to plant in me.
But I try so hard to fight
Against what I've learned
Then the peace of God comes,
And all the tables turned.
Jesus Christ can take it all,
My white brothers understand
How much I cry, there are so many
Tears in this black man.
How can you understand
Unless you've cried as a black man?
I don't want to sell drugs,
But my babies have to eat
I hear them cry, am I
Bleeding to death in the street?
God, God please come and save my life
What will happen to my sons and my wife?
How do I fix this? What do I do?
If my life is through, who can I turn to?
I get to my knees, begging Jesus please
Don't let me die before you tell me why.
I know in my heart that it's all my fault
And now my life is coming to a complete halt.
Help me God, use me like you used
Your ancient judges
Keep me safe and out of the devil's clutches.
I give it all to you God, please hear my scream

The blood on my clothes reminds me it's not a dream.
How can you understand
Unless you've cried as a black man?

Save Me Jesus

Save me Jesus, save me from hell
Save me Jesus, save me from myself.
He paid our ransom, so we could be free
He bought us, we're his and to live obediently.
We could have the world and lose our souls
If we rely on flesh and our faith grows cold.
Teach us to be people who praise your name
Draw us even closer to your Holy Ghost flame!
Your sheep hear your voice, you call them by name
Give them the power so your word is proclaimed.
Be ye holy, for holy is the Lord
Get on your knees, show him He's adored!
He is holy and righteous and true
Do unto others as you want it done to you!
Save me from the torture of dying in my sin
Save me from the fears that live without and within!
Save me Lamb of God, save me Lord Jesus
Save me for a purpose and to keep me righteous!
Save me Jesus, save me from the day
The church leaves the earth and Satan has his way.
Save me Lord, save me from on high
Save me Jesus, save me until I die.
I want to be white as snow, fallen freshly on a lake
I want to be unique, just like every snowflake.
And see the frozen water, that's waiting to thaw out
And nourish my soul, it's what grace is all about!
It's in a ready state, saved for us to receive
And love is in our hearts when we truly believe.
Save me Jesus, save me from the times
I suffer and I battle, inside my own mind.
We could have the world and lose our souls
If we rely on flesh and our faith grows cold.
He is holy and righteous and true
Do unto others as you want it done to you!
He paid our ransom, so we could be free

He bought us, we're his and to live obediently.
Save me Jesus, save me from hell
Save me Jesus, save me from myself.

Genuine Tears

I've got music in my heart,
it's all I want to do
Make a melody or rhyme
So pure it touches you.
I want to feel the beauty
That comes in every note
And share with the world
The feelings that I wrote.
I want to be a guest of honor
At a banquet in your name
And seek to find the truth
While others play the game.
Of trying to earn the money
That will give them all they need
Please let me have the music,
I will let them have the greed.
Keep it simple stupid,
I always remind myself
Remember why you do this,
It's not for self or wealth.
Keep it simple stupid,
Because the melody won't hide
If you write for a paycheck
Or with genuine tears in your eyes.

New Clothes

"I've never had new clothes before,"
Said the little boy, through the screen door
"I don't deserve them, you know."
I thought, none of us do, "let's go."
We found the store, a busy one,
Everyone getting their lists done
We found the boy some new clothes,
And then got ready to go.
He turned to me to say,
"Thank you, I enjoyed today"
Then as if to extend the dream,
I said, "Let's have ice cream!"
Never be afraid, take the time,
Show a love that never leaves the mind
Whether son, brother or little friend,
Give yourself and joy's never far behind!

Looking Back

It's hard to look back and feel with regret
To see goals and ambitions, that haven't been met.
Hard it is to see chances that you missed
To help someone turn their despair into gladness.
It's not guilt alone and I loathe my selfishness
That keeps me apart from the things I do best.
Listening and working to lift this person up
Help them on their way, if they're stuck in a rut.
By helping them out, I get more than I give
From the good that I feel, it's the right way to live.

Here For You

What can I do for you? To make your dreams come true?
What can I find to help give you peace of mind?
Where can I go to cause your face to glow?
Where can I be that you will remember me?
What promise can I make to ease your heartache?
What nice thing can I do to change your life for you?
What knowledge can I gain to take away your pain?
What poetry can I write to make you cry all night?
What wonders can I share to lift you in the air?
What things can I pray to improve your life today?
How much can I love you to make your dreams come true?
How much time can I spend so our joy will never end?
How many times can I win just to bring you the ribbon?
So many times I will be more than you think you see.
And I will be here for you!

We Are All To Blame (Columbine)

My heart is broken,
The truth is some are dead
We are all to blame,
Blood that flows is still red.
We went not noticing
That someone else in need
We forgot them, our quest,
Our self-centered greed.
Now we humbly need to pray,
Ask God to forgive us
See His plan is always good,
Let none stand against us.
We have been bought with a price,
Our precious Savior's blood
Now the payment has come due,
The world will soon be judged.
Too long the church has waited,
Sitting guilty, apathetic
Worrying about our issues,
Not saving souls, pathetic!
Well church, the trumpet sounded
And it's time to use our weapon
Constantly praying to God,
Only He can we depend on.
The purchased saints have learned it,
Now put it into action
And preach the gospel to this world,
Get rid of all distraction!
And repent for our own sin,
This time that we have lost waiting
Serve Jesus Christ who lives
And died sin's power abating.
Do not be afraid servants,
When the world indeed will hate you
They will thank you more when they realize,

God's promises are true!
Be of great courage and know,
The Holy Spirit is with you
Righteous needed, report for duty,
What will God have us do?

Paul's Story

Paul's story: to give to God all glory!
He began as a Roman and wicked to the core
He persecuted Christians, yeah,
He killed them just for sport.
Started sending Roman soldiers to
Hunt the Christians down
The Lord came, told him the truth,
He fell onto the ground!
The Lord spoke with power,
Why do you persecute me?
I will show you all the things,
You'll suffer for my glory.
He went blind for three days,
While walking down that road
The Christians still feared him,
They prayed unto the Lord.
Barnabus was his helper
And his encouraged him to do
Showing the other Christians
That he was one now too.
Timothy was like his son, a pastor,
One of God's own
Caring for the people
While the love of God is shown.
Started travelling through the empire,
He used to be admired
Was thrown into many prisons,
As he spoke, he was on fire.
They needed a real life Savior,
One to worship and obey
And to change all their behavior,
How the Lord is the only way.
He took four missionary journeys
To preach and teach the lost
Suffered shipwrecks, scorn and stonings,

Though high, he paid the cost.
To be the Lord's apostle,
Yet he still had all humility
He said, "I have been chosen,
Chief of sinners though I be!"
He wrote many church letters,
So they would get the picture
How it teaches all saints to act,
It became our holy scripture.
He was there with Steven, Paul said "die,"
The first church martyr
God showed him grace and suffering,
Paul was the first church starter.
He died went to God,
Who saved Paul from himself
Filled him with the Holy Spirit
To help save someone else.
Are you ready for the message
The word of God is true
God saved someone like Paul,
Just think what he'll do for you!

I'll Be There When Disaster Comes

I grew up in California, one day I woke up on the floor
I sat there, what hit me? An earthquake at 7.4.
Later I moved to Colorado and I woke one morning
To the noise of a refinery exploding without any warning.
I have been stuck in blizzards and left out in the rain
Near a cruise ship that caught on fire,
Even fell off of a train.
I was just outside Nairobi,
When they bombed our embassy
We cried and prayed to God
And asked Him how could this be?
I'm almost afraid to travel, for when I go somewhere
The disaster soon will follow as will bitter, sad despair.
So I stayed home and I prayed to heal this heart of mine
I see it happen again, fifteen dead at Columbine.
It's now so all around me, I'm in shock and full of fear
Is my disgrace that I don't help or pray enough to hear?
The wisdom of the Lord and all the hope He brings
I need to get on my knees, start confessing everything.
Am I to blame for terror? Am I the one who should
Pray all day and sing aloud, help everyone I could?
Please God, I'm hurting, this guilt is hard to bear
Forgive me God, my sin so large, my selfishness, despair.
What do you want me to do? I'm foolish in my lusts
Of all I want or think I need instead of just to trust.
I'm foolish Lord forgive me, I hate the bad I do
Please help me remind me, your promises are true.
I'll be there when disaster comes
And won't be afraid of them
I will be lead by God's Spirit and pray to ease their pain.
And find a purpose in serving, God and fellow man
Be more like the servant I am and do the best God can.

To Do Something Remarkable

Give me your children so I can teach them well
Teach them to love and not hate to
Be calm and contemplate.
Give me your hungry so I can feed them all
Feed them with compassion and hope,
Strength each day to cope.
Give me your cold so I can warm them all over
Warm them with truth
And clothes or heat from my stove.
Give me your hopeless so I can fill them up
Fill them with love and dignity, to be all they hope to be.
Give my your elderly so I can teach them to learn
Keep their brains and bodies working,
Where doubt and fear are lurking.
Give me your tired
And I will give them peaceful rest
I will tuck them in at night,
Tell them it is and will be all right.
Give me your misfits and I will find them a place
They'll be important and whole,
Content and happy in their soul.
Give me your wealthy and I will teach them humility
That life is more that what you acquire
Or fulfilling each desire.
Give me your poor and I will give them riches
Not ones of silver or gold,
But nourishment for their souls.
Give me your addicted and I will teach them control
Keep their hearts sincere,
So they won't live in constant fear.
Give me your heartless and I will give them emotion
So they can feel what they do
And learn it hurts them too.
Give me your arrogant so I can teach them fear
Change the way they act

And watch their selfishness subtract.
Give me this writer and I will give him a mission
Take away his distraction, so he can call you to action.
So he will make you think and he will move your heart
Steal your apathy or sloth so you will pay the cost,
To do something remarkable.

When I'm Dead

No more tears to shed, no more tasks to dread
No more getting out of bed, when I'm dead.
No more some things I must do or eating out with you
No more deciding what to do when I'm worm food.
No more getting old and gray, no more bills I have to pay
No more cloudy or sunny days, when I start to decay.
No more smiles that I can see, or friends that I try to be
No more debating philosophy when I'm set free.
No more hatred in my heart, no more spending time apart
No more projects left to stop or start when I depart.
No more love that I can share, no more going anywhere
No more ways to show I care, this life is so rare.

Ask My Savior

Ask my Savior what He wants me to be
He'll say a martyr hanging on a tree.
Ask my savior, King of Kings and love
He'll send His power, brought high from above.
Look unto Jesus, tell me who you see
A humble servant, peaceful and mighty.
His love will surround you, His spirit sets you free
Look into His eyes, you'll see eternity.
Ask my savior what he thinks of you
He'll say you're precious, more precious that jewels
Ask my savior, who is made of love
He'll give you power, brought from above

No Father, No Son

No father, no son, I'm left alone and undone
No wisdom, no joy, just me, my heart destroyed.
No brothers to help defend, I'm solitary to the end
No freedoms, no choice, little time left to rejoice.
No baseball games or weddings,
Just time alone I'm dreading
No father, no son, more questions still to come.
What did I do, what have I said
To create doubt in my head
I've always hoped for a dream come true.
A father for me and a son, someone to teach
Hold and guide, to carry on when I have died.
What do I do or where do I go from here?
A lifetime alone and that loneliness brings fear.
To find a dad, to bring a son,
To one alone and all undone
Where can I turn, to change my fate?
Oh my God, is it too late?

The Things I Say

The canvas I paint on is white,
The brush is simple and light
The colors I use are so bright,
So refreshing when brought in your sight.
The pictures I paint are with words,
The subjects are sometimes absurd
Because I live to soar like a bird,
The things I say can be heard.
I teach you how to trust,
I write about inner feelings and lusts
The words can help you adjust,
Or disappear like the dust.
Poems can point out beauty,
Not written like fulfilling a duty
Presented to the world so truly,
Spoken as an act of purity.
My hope is to reach your heart,
Examinations not kept on a chart
And as your desperation departs,
Only then can the healing start.

Bride of Haarlem

A tree white as snow,
Known as the Bride of Haarlem
It was fifty-seven years ago,
When the bombs first came
We went out to meet the Germans,
We were strong but innocent
They came with tanks and guns,
Quickly our courage went.
They started out with labels, rations and ID cards
Life was little change at first, soon it was too hard.
Our Jewish neighbors would disappear
We all knew the answer inside
They were taken to Auschwitz or worse
And six million of them died.
It's a sad thing to remember how
The world allowed this all to occur
When evil reigned and God seemed too busy
Hope was all we had to help us endure.
Little Holland seemed so safe
But tyranny knows no borders
A world gone mad, when death and
Torture, are only following orders.

Testimony

I grew up in a house where love didn't live
It was all take and rarely any give.
My dad didn't love me, he didn't care
Mom searching for love that wasn't there.
Dad used to love to drink and smoke tobacco
Made him quiet, made him mad even wacko.
Mom and I moved out she found a new man
He was abusive and drank too, bad plan.
Moved to Colorado and it was raining
I remember seeing the sky and complaining.
Years of chemical abuse around me
Soon I was abusing too, so naturally.
My life took off in the wrong way
Good grades, good drugs all child's play.
Then we moved again, mom found a new man
An ex-marine with a gun in his hand.
He acted somewhat charming,
You would never know
How bad agent orange was taking control.
He had seizures, fits and pain in his head
Seven years after I met him, I heard he was dead.
So I went to college to gain more knowledge
It was a high class school and I played the fool.
I went from books to doing more drugs
I had to hang out with my homey thugs.
So they kicked me out, I was mad
I went to California to see my real dad.
He kicked me out over using the phone
Just a dumb fight and me without a home.
So I lived in the park, cold after dark
A little girl said ,"where do you live", where do I live?
I came back home, met a girl, changed my world
Followed her to Kansas City, she wasn't too pretty.
Are we gonna have a baby, well maybe baby
Her eyes got wild and she killed my child!

I was as low as I could get, a mental emotional wreck
Then I was walking in the rain,
Where they thought me insane.
Started talking to God, didn't know what else to do.
Started telling Him my story and with all His glory
He showed me another way and taught me how to pray.
Now I knew I had to go back home to Colorado
Got there Christmas eve, I belong, why did I leave?
So God brought a friend to me, sweet as a honey bee
She said yes I asked to be, in her life for eternity
God has a plan and it's good for you
Ask him how, He will see you through.
He can wash away all the hurt inside
Like He did for me when he came into my life.
His holy power can set you free
Make you complete like He did for me.
Teach you to give, love and forgive
Live life the way you ought to live.
His gift of life, yes it is free
And it will last for eternity.
Jesus Christ died on the cross
To show the devil who's really boss.
Paid the price for all your sin
Opened heaven so you can come in
Accept His son and the price he paid
To protect your soul you've got to get saved.

Don't Kill Me Daddy

Don't kill me daddy, I'm a part of you
Mommy don't you love me, I live inside you too.
Someday I'll live in your world and run free
Please let me live to be the child
You're supposed to see.
I know you love me, I love you too
If you love me let me live, anywhere will do.
I don't want to be a statistic, my heart beats inside
Lifelong regrets and constant pain await you if I die.
God isn't ready for me, I have a life to live
Your my vessel and my hope, it's my birth please give.
If you can't take care of me, or just don't want to
I know somewhere someone will, anywhere will do.
My eyes are so innocent, my future so unsure
You have a choice, choose me, I'm still pure.
Please let me live, I should not be here
Fighting for my life in the place I feel secure.
Please don't kill me daddy, I have your eyes
Fight for me mommy, don't believe the lies.
I'm inconvenient, but cute, 10 fingers and 10 toes
I'll change your whole world
When you watch me grow.
Go ahead and have me, I'll try to be good
I only ask a chance to live, is that understood?

Donna's Story

A moment filled with regret, a moment full yet grim
Saying no this once was wrong, but I went to find him.
He was surprised to see me then a smile filled his face
He warmed my heart, inside his eyes were filled with grace.
He took the ribs, said thanks, then off into the night
I took the time, I'm glad I did, the thing I knew was right.
My heart's for helping others, my love is not misguided
Some people don't understand, sometimes I get chided.
But love rises above that, and it grows inside my heart
For great things to be done through me
And this only the start.

Dreams Pass Away

Dreams pass away, like a time yet to come
When the words left to say, are left alone.
Deep in this heart mine, there will come the time
For the chance to shine and a love so eager to find.
Passion alone, can convert a stone
And a taste of more to come
Filled with the bliss, from one lovers kiss
And wanting nothing more than this
Living life in a way, that you're proud of today
No chances left to take
Heart on a string, a new world to bring
Closer to, the love, that grows.
Dreams pass away, like a time yet to come
When the words left to say, are left alone.

Kitty's Song

Pieces of me on the carpet, pieces of me on the chair
Pieces of me are everywhere, and not just my hair.
It's my heart you remember, it's the way I love you
The time I feel most important, like my dreams came true.
I must go . . . on to the end
My life has been better, you were my friend.
Not just a friend, closer, spoken words unspoken
Like a strong bond, that cannot be broken.
Pieces of me on the carpet, I'm sorry for the mess
And all the other times you know I must confess.
I couldn't have been in a nicer place,
I'm glad you were mine
As I sit here and ponder, it is now my time.
Don't weep for me now, I am more than glad
For the time we spent together, please, don't be sad.
I must go . . . on to the end
My life has been better, you were my friend.

Own Feelings

I choose my own feelings, I feel how I want to feel
I can control my own dealings, in everything I am real.
How you see me, may not always be
The way I am nor the way I should be.
But I'm human too, sometimes things happen
As quick as a wink or two fingers snapping.
Remember, we're all emotional, some show it more often
Others guard it well until they rest in a coffin.
Feelings, sometimes they hurt, sometimes they heal
Sometimes just a burden always true and real.

Light In My World

There's a light in my world, since you turned it on
There's more blue in the sky, when loneliness is gone.
All fun is the start in matters of the heart
Feeling pretty smart and cannot stand to be apart.
Then reality comes in, still a game you can win
All you do then to begin, to fall deeper in love again.
There's a light in my world, so brightly it burns
With the triumph of love and the feelings we learn.
We take love inside us, it changes every place
Full of hatred or filth, everywhere that needs replaced.
It fills us up with power, it finds us where we are
It never makes us sorry, that we had to come so far.

Peace

Peace is not easy to find in this world of ours
It is the main cause of many of our wars
Wars are started to try and preserve peace
But once they've started, they never seem to cease.
Peace is intangible, peace to us is unknown
A stranger in the distance, peace can never be shown
Once peace is found, it seems something occurred
Like it is out of our imagination,
Like it's something you've heard
We know it's only a dream, peace can never be found
As long as men live together on God's sacred ground
If we eliminate ourselves, there is peace for all the rest
But how can there be peace with death's emptiness
Peace is a word spoken without an easy breath
Peace is serenity, but serenity is death . . . .

Never Entered The Truth

The restless life
Wishing, fishing for a dream
Missing, knowing what's in between
No one has been where I've been.
Dying, trying for no one else but me
Losing, using everything that I see
Binding, finding trouble looms ahead
Would I be better off dead?
Searching, lurching forward on a dime
Seeking, speaking and wasting time
Living, giving handouts to the poor
What else could be in store?
Burning, turning off and on again
Feeling healing from one drop of rain
Seeing, being what I wanted most to be
Then a change came over me.
There was a time I didn't know you
Into my mind never entered the truth
About your love and what that could mean
From far above where it once was a dream.
Nobody told me then, how could I know
About the promise of heaven, the fire down below.
You came and told the stories that are true
Now I'm getting old, am I supposed to be with you?
I walked with you alone and all you did was listen
I was far away from home
And knew something was missing.
You brought me off the ground
And guided through the rain
I started to seek you and found,
My life made sense again.

Gathers His Own

Our God is unfailing
He's always around
With His creative beauty
Sights, smells and sounds
Our Father is with us
Enables our growth
He waits patiently
And draws us so close
In the hearts of His children
A new hope still grows
Like the bright part of heaven
The heavenly throne
Sits the Father
Who gathers His own.

Cloudy Skies

Humble through thy forbidden night
See the colors remove our fright
Anxiously awaiting for dawning light
How can we decide what's right?
Everlasting openness in song or in tune
Begin to end loneliness, the rising moon.
Resist destruction life long friends
Sunrise construction, sun setting ends.
Journeys forever, momentary peace
Meaningless if ending without release.

For The Love Of God Won't Wait

Guided by strength, driven by the will to exist
Taking great lengths, able to persist.
Crushed under the militants rule,
Caused to abandon so much
Taking lessons from the old school,
Longing for freedoms touch.
Feelings of damnation, how shall we survive?
Reducing our nation, just to stay alive.
Through all the strife and death and pain
Shines Jesus Christ, coming soon again
So many blessings to receive
For God's children who believe.
Let us not be too sedate
For the love of God won't wait
The feast is waiting on our plates
Let's give thanks and open the gates.
God had so much love did He
He sent his Son to die for me
That I will live eternally
Jesus did this willingly.
I shall never be afraid
Look at all that God has made
All that is seen and unseen
Mountain tops and valleys green.
If I only give my heart
Jesus is a brand new start
We shall never be apart
Let God play the biggest part.
In the daily life we live
To ourselves and neighbors give
All the love that God provides
Let His kingdom come alive.

Joseph's Song

I'm head over heels for you Mary
In your womb is your son
Though I'm not his father I love you both
And my love has only begun.
In time we'll be a family
Together on this earthen sod
What a surprise! In a dream an angel
Told me He is the Son of God.
His name is Jesus
What a beautiful boy, no fears
His heart has love and peace
And wisdom beyond his years.
How can I raise the Son of God
He should be teaching me the way
Sons someday leave their fathers
I dread the coming of that day
What will He be like?
How will He change our world
I'm just a simple carpenter
Why am I so honored? So bold?
Everyday, the shadow of the cross
Will be there to remind him
Even I, an earthly father
Put him there for my sin . . . .

Catfish Are Great Listeners

You may think they're all washed up,
Nothing but whiskers and gills
But here's something that you should
Know among your many thrills
Catfish are great listeners,
They're all eyes and ears
You know that when you speak to them,
Your words they really hear
When talking to an aardvark,
Or a worldly wise old owl
It seems they don't always hear my words,
Distracted, distant somehow
So converse with a cheerful catfish,
But not when he's your main dish
And don't expect an answer either,
After all he's just a fish.

Revelation 'Round The Mountain

He'll be riding a white horse when He comes
He's called Faithful and True and righteous judge
With a vesture dipped in blood,
His name is called the word of God
He reigns forever KING OF KINGS
AND LORD OF LORDS Amen!
To the seven churches, grace and peace
From Him who was and is and is to come
Comfort from the seven spirits, and from
Christ the faithful witness
The first born of the dead and King of Kings.
Behold for He is coming with the clouds
And every eye will see Him, every one
Everyone who pierced Him, all the tribes of earth will
Wail because of Him. Even so. Amen.
I am the Alpha and Omega says the Lord
Who is and was and is to come Almighty
John our brother saw this vision,
On a island called Patmos
Here's the word and testimony of Jesus Christ.
John heard a loud voice say write what you see
In the spirit on the Lord's Day was he
He turned to see the voice,
And saw seven golden lamp stands
One like the son of man was in their midst.
He was clothed with a long white robe
His head and hair were white like wool or snow
His eyes a flame of fire, His feet like burnished bronze
And his voice like the sound of many waters.
In his right hand he held seven stars
A sharp two-edged sword came from his mouth
And He shone like the sun, in all his strength and glory
I fell at his feet like I was dead.

Dangers Come To Stay

Oh gracious God, when danger's come to stay
In silence I whisper, beseech you and pray
Knees on the floor, scars there from before
Clinging to the Lord, because His love is pure.
One more sinner seeking wisdom
One more heart that will unfold
And after all the Lord is right here waiting
He knocks we open up the door.
Satan is waiting to try and trip you up
Offers you evil and sin and your own demise
Tries to crack your armor, hang on, to the Lord
His power's made perfect in you,
His grace will keep you whole.
Look at all the lonely people
Who spend their lives lost and alone
We have the word to help their eyes to open
Then the love of God is shown.
One more sinner seeking wisdom
One more heart that will unfold
And after all the Lord is right here waiting
He knocks we open up the door.

Say A Prayer To The Lord

Say a prayer to the Lord, to the Savior Son
Grace and peace kingdom come
Bringing all of the world to the end of strife
In a cloud he will come.
Pray with your heart open,
Telling Him all that's inside
Jesus Christ, saved my life
Took my sin, now I'm clean and whole again!
Suffered pain, suffered death,
He was raised again to give sinners a chance
Healed the sick raised the dead,
But for Him instead
We yelled," Crucify Him!"
Pray with your heart open,
Telling Him all that's inside
Jesus Christ, saved my life
Took my sin, now I'm clean and whole again.
Faith is more than speaking the words
Pour your heart out to the Lord
You will find His grace will suffice
Keep you pure and sanctified.
Jesus Christ, saved my life
Now I'm His! What a gracious God He is!

Soldiers Unknown

*"Here Rests in Honored Glory an
American Soldier Known But to God"*
   engraving, Tomb of the Unknown Soldier

They gave the ultimate gift to us
Their lives for our freedom
Their sacrifice was to never taste
Freedom's blessings to come.
Everyday hassles we all endure
Little problems that come and go
They would gladly trade their place
With us, to lay our complaining low.
Freedom's price is very high
Forgetting's price is even greater
So many veterans ignored and lonely
Their eyes growing dim as each day gets later.
Mass graves mean anonymous death
From Guadalcanal to Hanoi
The German Front to Pearl Harbor
All American mothers have lost a boy.
Inside and out they carried scars
Freedom's price they paid to share
The kinds of things you can never understand
Unless you too have been there.
General Douglas MacArthur once said,
"Old soldiers never die-they just fade away."
Our merciful God has a special reward
To those chosen-the ultimate price to pay!

Dedicated to those who fought for us and died for us. I'm sorry we never got to say thank you or goodbye in person. Rest In Peace Brothers and Sisters. God Bless You All.

So We Could Learn Of Love

Writing our names in the sand,
Two young lovers holding hands
When the light came on, we grew strong,
So we could learn of love.
Sharing a glass like lovers do,
Sharing our thoughts, just me and you
The closer we become, the less I run,
Now we can walk in love.
Watching the love light up your eyes,
no more searching through the skies
Walk the road together, now and forever,
Someday we'll marry love.
Take this ring and take my heart,
Love remains right from the start
Now we have no fear, thoughts are clear,
We'll always be in love.
Having kids and spending time,
I am yours and you are mine
With the love of God, the love of God,
We teach the world to love.
Thinking back in time my dear,
Passing through another year
Remembering the glance, we took a chance,
And found forever love.

My Mother's Other Son

Best wishes to you and God bless you too
You're lucky to have each other, one another
Rare is a love that you find and keep
And rarer the thoughts I share this deep.
Celebrations make me feel crazy and sad
While remembering the past, all that was bad
I wish I could change, at least rearrange
Things done such and such, before I knew this much.
But forward we go and yet work is hard to find
I've got to find work before I lose my mind
But I guess a year is not so long to wait
It's been this long without a clean slate
You are always welcome to see me again
Let me know you're coming and I'll let you in
You can stay at my place, it's real small & no bed
But I would like to see you in my homestead
Surprising- how comfortable the floor
Come by before seven, that's when they lock the doors
Bring a blanket, brother, because I only have one
Hope to see you soon, my mother's other son.

Each, Alone Must Choose

I sit in my room facing doubt and gloom
I look at our state and it's not great
We Americans are again at war
This one will last- it's a war with our past
Lost in the tattered ashes where memories remain
Are the subtle, nagging realities of pain
We have a world that doesn't love anymore
One that's ready to take and take more
One that is busy finding new ways to show hate
And one that is already sealed in it's fate
We once punished people for the color of their skin
And sunk ourselves deeper into our pitiful sin
We've allowed mothers to kill their children unknown
And left in their stead empty hearts and empty homes
We found that our bombs became easier to drop
And end many lives, is it ever going to stop?
A graduation to bullets is where our hate has grown
And everyone's so busy that we all end up alone
I've gotten no hope from this world where I reside
Will I do good or evil? Each, alone must decide
Will I take myself out for a steak and a beer?
Or take out my heart to let someone come near?
Will I look at the stars and cry? Or will I
See someone in need instead of passing them by?
This world is no good, but this place here, my heart
Lies a vast untapped resource, a good place to start
Here in this place where emotion lives well
It's a piece of my soul and my life not for sale
I know nothing more than this world needs a change
Can I do? Shall I go? I don't know, it's so strange!
I can look at my brothers and join in their mania
Or send Mariamu some help, she's in Tasmania
Or help someone here in my own corner of the globe
With a meal or a hug or some kindness I've shown
Or be like we all are-greedy, selfish, and wrong
Each, alone must choose, just don't wait too long.

The Thread

Woven through the fabric of our lives
It's the thread of love we share
Brings us closer and lets us
Show how much we care.
The thread is stretched tight
Beautiful it comes to life
Bringing hearts close and sharing time
Letting true love take flight.
Brought forth to stitch our seams
Tie our hearts and share our dreams
Much is made of the color scheme
Yellow, blue, black, red and green.
Thread is quite fragile, delicate at best
Binding the cord with more threads
Watch the love pass the test
Helps us all into unity to be lead.

From My Window

Holes in the window, blanket by the door
Splinters in the wall and the floor
Looks like another winter storm
Wonder if I'll stay warm?
Bills are hard to pay
But I can watch TV
Watch all the pretty people
Who buy and sell me.
Talking about some way
To give us people help
Then sending millions to
Rainforests, fungus or kelp.
I'm not against the trees
Or the animals or bugs
But I'd like to live in a place that's
Warm and not overrun with drugs.
A place where I can say my prayers
Not live and freeze in fright
A place where I can look forward
To, not dread each coming night.
But power people play their games
And I alone am left
To die in my bed alone and cold
Without love or respect.

The Battle

The torch is lit, lights are on
Pounding drums make rhythm go
Feet seem to move on their own
This is the beginning of the show
As the night grows darker still
Whether hunting heads or hearts
The fire will eventually find you
And it only takes a spark!
The words are spoken out loud
Telling an old story of truth past
Where all the world that is will be
Gone forever; that time comes fast
Battling the witch doctor on his
Own battlefield right here
All the villagers gather around
And trembling with fear
They watch and wait and wonder
Who has the strongest god
Whether demons or the Lord of
Lords will rule on their sod
Evil strikes the first blow
And sin is running wild
While good sits back and bides
Time waiting the birth of one child
Not just any child you see
But the only Son of love
Who left His crown upon His throne
When He came here from above
With His mighty suit of armor
Righteousness and truth is He
All the demons know His name
And as they should, they flee
"You have no place or purpose here!"
His thundering voice did say
"Be cast into the lake of fire

For all your wicked ways"!
And while we too should be there
Through His love and His grace
His own Son's blood sacrifice
We can see him face to face
As long as we ask forgiveness
And seek to be redeemed
We can live in a place more
Beautiful than any we could dream.

Jappy And Me

I have a friend, I don't know well yet
We work for the same boss and we never forget
Our purpose in life is to touch our youth
We teach them with hope, we reach them with truth.
What we have inside makes us true brothers
With a heavenly Father and a different mother
Our hearts are for Jesus and His reign of peace
Sharing with a friend a love that doesn't cease.
We found each other before both God and men
We prayed for each other and then prayed again
When that event was over we said stay in touch
We cried our eyes out because we loved so much.
And we wanted to show how love breaks down walls
Like my skin color or age and other pitfalls
So we stand here as partners with a love growing strong
We work hard for Jesus as we should all along.
And we hope to be together though we're miles apart
We share a destination with the one in our hearts
It makes all the difference when a friend's there to share
And our wives see us better when our brother is there.
We all need a brother who shares the same need
To love and to serve and to share and to bleed
Red blood of courage for doing what's right
And lifting up brothers in prayer each night.
Making a difference in the lives that we touch
Showing the world that our God is our crutch
He's the one we cling onto tighter each day
Because He cared enough to take our sin away.

Two Way Street

Why is God so lonely sitting on His throne
With a universe full of love and He's there all alone
His heart is wide open and calling out to me
Because all I do lately is done just for me.
He doesn't want a minute or an hour or a day
He wants our minds to put Him first in all we do or say
But He doesn't make us do it no love does not use force
Yet He finds a way to everyone
And helps them chart a course.
That leads right back to Him and His loneliness can end
When we accept the gifts He gives
And accept Him like a friend
For everyone is lonely and God is lonely too
Sitting there near Eden's gate and waiting just for you.
And patiently He sits and waits, a day, a month or a year
And hears the sound of every sigh,
Sees the flow of every tear
And loneliness it comes and goes
And God is still there waiting
Graciously He deals in love and never deals in hating.
Loneliness a two way street, do you think that God is there?
Do you wonder if He misses you? Do you realize He cares?
So help yourself and help him too and you will plainly find
The peace, the joy, the love that comes
When you look into God's mind.

As Midnight Strikes

Cold room so very dark and deep
With only a toilet and a place to sleep
Endless hours spent all alone
Crying so hard, I can't breathe but groan.
My life didn't have to be this way
Just one thing I did, one time, one day
Put me here in this six by ten
Where death comes hourly, it's coming again.
I never meant to do bad or make others lives sad
And I'm full in my heart of regrets
Time passes while paying my debt.
But in the depth of this pit,
When all I can do is quit
I'm suddenly aware, someone else is there.
It's not a person, in this place
But the Spirit of God full of grace
And He reaches to me to love
Sharing what I'm not worthy of.
He's here, "but why?" I ask Him
He says, "I've always been here Jim
I've loved you every step of the way
That's why I've come here today.
Your life here will soon end,
I want you to know my friend
That I love you everyday,
And I hope that you will say:
I love you too God and
I'm sorry for what I've done
And please forgive my sins
From the blood of Christ your Son."
"Oh God! I am sorry
But how can I believe
You would come to save my
Soul this night and offer this reprieve."
It's two minutes to midnight

God I take your truth in
"I know my evil ways are wrong
I'm sorry for my sin.
Please take me home to heaven
And into your holy rest
Though I don't deserve it
Please do Lord, what is best!"
Now I've made my peace Lord
And I see the holy lights
No more will death row be my home
The clock sounds, as midnight strikes!

Does She Get

Does she get a kiss on the cheek
Or the kind of kiss where she can't even speak?
Does she get a kiss on the hand
Or the kind of kiss that's more than she planned?
Does she get a man on his knees to
Ask her the words that her heart has dreamed?
Does she get a ring on her finger
And incredible roses that he would bring her?
Does she get a man of his word to hold her
And keep her safe in this world?
Does she get a baby inside her
From a man who is gentle and a good provider?
Does she get to stay home with her kid
And love him and care for, like her mother did?
Does she get to cry on that day
When the school bus comes and takes him away?
Does she feel proud as she watches him grow
And sees him learn what he needs to know?
Does she still love the man of her dreams,
When a new baby comes and its first words are screams?
Does she feel trapped by the life that she chose or,
Love that husband with the big nose even more?
Does she feel happy when her son goes to college,
As they save and they help him to gain more knowledge?
Does she feel sad when he graduates and says,
"Mom, there's this girl and we've set a wedding date."
Does she feel alone as they walk down the aisle
With hope in their hearts and wearing big smiles?
Someday she may have to lay him to rest,
And cry so hard, the ground will get wet.
She'll always remember the day that they met
And his love is powerful, she'll never forget.
He does so many things to show how he cares,
Serving her and he lifts her up in prayer.
He asks God to keep her holy and pure,

To strengthen their love so they will be sure.
They pray for protection and peace,
So the love God has built will never cease.
This is my prayer if you're married too,
Trust in the Lord and he'll bring you through.
In this world where the hazards are all that we see,
Remember, His love is real and makes us free.

Don's Legacy & Story

They truly love him, in many ways he cared
He had a heart of gold and laughter he shared.
Went about in a simple way the life he was given
Heather's crying tears on her way back to Lincoln.
Tears have stained the bed where he had laid
Hearts still unfolding with the memories they made.
The haven their home was will be different somehow
And horseback riding with grandpa
Is only a memory now.
You both shared equal love, interest and attention
Making us feel important with a personal connection.
Flash that smile one more time so we can see Jesus in you
Comfort us with God's own love as we're torn in two.
You taught us laughter and were a kind and gentle spirit
With the words we needed and close
Enough so we would hear it.
You cared about animals,
Especially that mule, old cinnamon
And stopped to watch the eagles
Soar above you in the wind.
Now we must learn to be as
Passionate about life as you were
It's hard to learn without the
Master to show us, we are sure.
But we thank God that you came
And we got to know you
And all you did to teach us love,
You made our dreams come true.

Sun Lee's Story

You see me with a limp
And think I'm a nobody here
The land mine did this and
It's certainly not my idea.
I wasn't born this way,
But everyday I must endure it
My people fought over a speck of dirt,
Bombs used to procure it.
I'm glad I'm in America and
There is no more war, yes it's tough
Even though I'm crippled, I survived,
And most days that's enough.

Spongy Lungs

I have spongy lungs,
They hardly weigh a pound
They get the air into me
And my blood takes it around.
It's all in working order, but I'm ready for a rest
People tell me I'm lucky, I've been given all the best.
That's true, you know, I guess,
But it hasn't all been great
Everyday I'm just happy to have food on my plate.
The absurdity of fools is near,
They laugh at wisdom instead
Choosing folly and bringing disaster upon their heads.
Prosperity comes when you're willing to repent
To receive the gift of eternal life that He has sent.
Get involved and be committed to serving God each day
When you're lost or falling apart, He will light your way.
Fear, obey, love and serve and your faith will grow
Pray, seek, believe and trust and
God will make you whole.
Seek each day to spend some time to be
With God, your devotion
In a quiet place where you can share
Without the world's commotion.

Stars That Shine

I began as a lonely child, searching for the truth
All the wishes I didn't dare, to whisper have come true.
I realize that the stars shine, even if I don't see
So it is with the love of God, always there for me.
He guides me through the night,
Everyday He's by my side
I will choose to walk with Him, a safer place to abide.
Following the narrow path, can be a lonely way
But I prefer it to a broader road, one that leads astray.
Take a chance, see the light, search for something more
Listen closely to hear the sound,
He knocks on your heart's door.
I began as a lonely child, searching for the truth
All the wishes I didn't dare, to whisper have come true.
Take a chance, the narrow path,
Guiding me throughout the night
Always there, so listen close and see the stars that shine.
I realize that the stars shine, even if I don't see
So it is with the love of God, always there for me.

Voices On The River

Voices clearly on the river from a long time ago
I hear the children's laughter as I watch the river flow.
I hear the sage wisdom of a grandpa with his brood
I feel the tension melt as the river cures my mood.
I see an ancient warrior giving his horse a drink
I sit here and I listen, pondering as I think.
I think about a rafter on their first trip through the rocks
The coolness of water, on my feet no shoes or socks.
I hear the whistle blowing as a train begins it climb
And I hope the trout will bite as I tease them with my line.
Voices on the river, I hear them all today
Even as I go to sleep they still have more to say.
Watch me daddy! Look here comes a kayak
Throw the frisbee mommy and the dog brings it back.

Just A Dream

Look into the past, look into the future
A question of certainty, creates a feeling unsure.
Anticipation, searching through the scenes,
Mass confusion from both of the extremes.
Peaceful tranquility, early in the dawn
Sound invasion, as the night comes along.
Mountain nectar flowing in the streams
Just passing by, the twilight of a dream.
Over the hills and through green pastures
Relaxing on a stump, conversation with the Master.
Above the tree tops, like a bird so it seems
Awakening I realize, it was only but a dream.

Seed Of Knowledge

I've now reached a point, that I never thought I'd reach
When I've learned all I can, and am forced now to teach.
The knowledge I've gained in my few short years
Is good enough I believe for all ears to hear.
The struggle for power and the right to be free
Pieces of the puzzle that are locked inside me.
Locked in they will stay until mankind learns to be
Caring and sharing and live in harmony.
Life called the great puzzle, some pieces are now gone
While the search for their mystery continues on.
The reasons are so simple, if people could only see
The sensible answer that 's locked inside me.
If I am the knowledge and you are the spirit
We can join together for others to hear it.
The puzzle fits together, so perfect and precise
Plant the seed now and we'll be back on the rise.
The future's now before us, coming into view
The followers are mislead, but I know what to do.
To plant the seed of knowledge and give it time to grow
If we can work together, who knows?

The Roadhouse Grill

Like a beacon in the distance
That was the Roadhouse Grill
After twenty days of traveling
I didn't need any thrills.
I could smell the meatloaf cooking
Fried potatoes are ready now
A piece of pie for dessert
And coffee, what great chow!
It's not some fancy diner
Or a greasy spoon to go
It's a place that feels like home
When you live life on the road.
There's Mabel waiting on tables
Joey's making up orders to go
Lucy's talking on the phone again
To her best friend Emma Jo.
I like to drop in and sit awhile
Whenever I'm in the neighborhood
They treat me like I'm family
And you know, the food is real good.

My Heart Is Open

My heart is open, it's burning, it's bleeding
It's yearning, it's pleading to
Ease the pain, again
My mouth is open, it's speaking, it's singing
It's shrieking, it's bringing,
Friends, closer together
My mind is open, it's pondering, and it's zooming
It's wandering, it's grooming,
A plan, to save this land
My ears are open, they're hearing, they're sharing
They're endearing, they're caring
About you, for all of you
My hands are open, they're touching, they're feeling
They're clutching, they're healing,
The tears, shed this year
The door is always open, it's swinging, it's flinging
Wide open, and I'm hoping, you'll drop by
And spend some time with me.

The Benediction

May the Lord protect and defend you
Make His face shine on and be gracious to you
May He find you worthy,
May He keep you healthy, too.
God is righteous and is not evil
His glory shines, through all His people
In all His creation, He has made
perfection mine, and yours.
My God can do great things for He is mighty
Worthy to be praised, holy, worthy
Filled with grace abundant,
Overflowing to me, it is free.
Once lost in sin, He has saved me
I'm glad He's made me whole from what could be
He found me, I was down,
I will wear a crown to reign, with him.
I have spent my life seeking answers
Heard rumors of the truth, but never answers
Now He has come in,
Washed away my sin for His glory.
Now I want to be but a servant
A peasant or a slave, His lowly servant
Making others better,
Always seeking what truth is, in Him.
Would you like to walk in His footsteps
Walk the long hard road in his footsteps
Those He calls His own,
Never walk alone for He, is there.
Gather round the cross there on Calvary
The place where love was shown to humanity
If we bear the cross, we will not be lost for He, is God.
May the Lord protect and defend you
Make his face shine on and be gracious to you
May He find you worthy,
May He keep you healthy too. He loves you.

Author Biography

Rick Roberts was born and raised in Los Angeles, California before moving to Denver in 1974. Rick has been a member of the Colorado Press Association since 1998. He has numerous magazine, newspaper and local publication writing credits including the Denver Post and Rocky Mountain News. This is his thirteenth poetry book since 1995. His passion is people and the interesting stories that go with them. His life is one of redemption and hope and is played out in the words that he writes. His desire is to know peace and joy more intimately and to share it with others.

Rick is currently a freelance filmmaker and photographer. His hobbies include playing music and singing, reading and traveling. His lives in Denver with his wife and two sons, you can contact Rick for more information at legacygrace@live.com.

Favorite Quote:
"He who looks inside his own heart dreams, he who looks outside his own heart awakens." Carl Jung

Books by Pearn and Associates, Inc.

The Bone Hunters, Thom Hatch

The Dreamer and the Dream, Rick E. Roberts

Black 14, Ryan Thorburn

Mathematics in Color, Joseph J. Kozma

A Lenten Journey Toward Christian Maturity, William Breslin

Walking in Snow, John Knoepfle

I look Around for my Life, John Knoepfle

Ikaria: A Love Odyssey on a Greek Island, Anita Sullivan

The U Book: Photo Travel Journal in India, Nathan Pierce

Another Chance, Joe Naiman

Goulash and Picking Pickles, Louise Mae Hoffmann

Point Guard, Victor Pearn

Printed in the United States
221877BV00002B/2/P